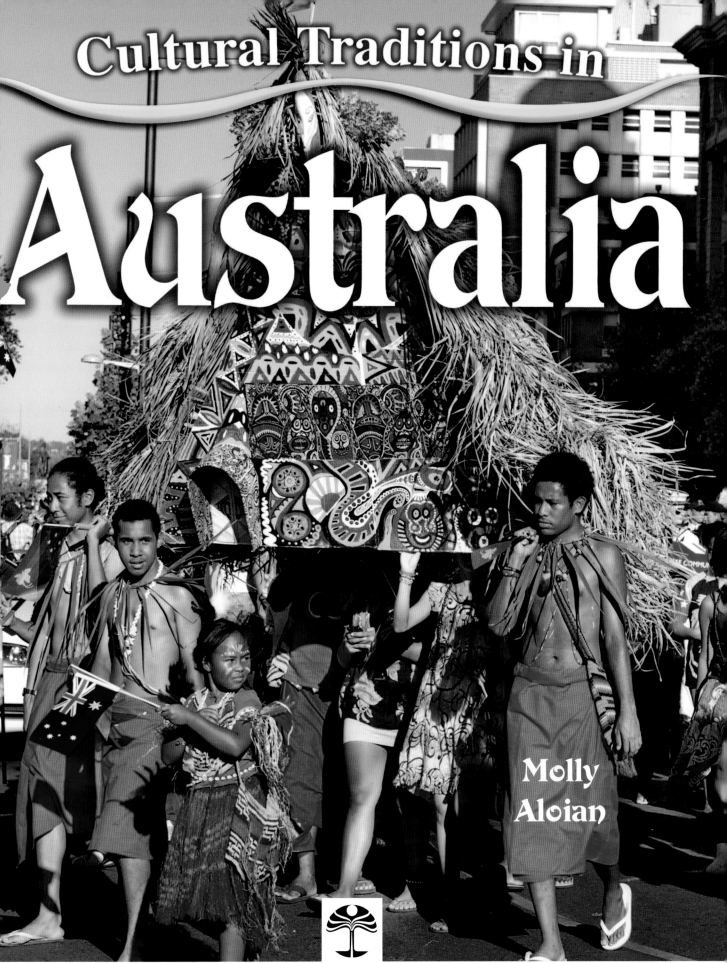

Cultural Traditions in
Australia

Molly
Aloian

Crabtree Publishing Company
www.crabtreebooks.com

Crabtree Publishing Company

www.crabtreebooks.com

Author: Molly Aloian
Publishing plan research and development:
Sean Charlebois, Reagan Miller
Crabtree Publishing Company
Project coordinator: Kathy Middleton
Editors: Adrianna Morganelli, Crystal Sikkens
Photo research: Crystal Sikkens
Design: Margaret Amy Salter
Production coordinator: Margaret Amy Salter
Prepress technician: Margaret Amy Salter
Print coordinator: Katherine Berti

Cover: Ayers Rock (background top); Aboriginal wooden mask (center); golden wattle (top left and right); kangaroo (middle left); Aboriginal folk dancer (middle right); Sydney Opera House (bottom center); fairy bread (bottom right); Australian meat pie with sauce (bottom left)

Title page: Aboriginal participants march in a Australia Day parade.

Photographs:
Alamy: Bill Bachman: page 23 (bottom); Ozimages: page 31
Ahn Young-joon/Associated Press: page 12
Captain Cook taking possession of New South Wales, c.1910 (colour litho), Gilfillan, John Alexander (1793-1867) (after) / Private Collection / The Bridgeman Art Library
Dreamstime:Rosedarc: pages 17 (bottom), 21; Andesign101: page 25; Dancantero: pages 28–29
iStockPhoto: cloudytronics: page 15 (bottom); Kokkai Ng: page 27 (top)
Shutterstock: cover (bottom left and middle), pages 7 (top), 11 (top and middle), 18 (right); Jack. Q: cover (middle right); Lev Kropotov: title page, page 26; Ingvars Birznieks: page 5; Atlaspix: page 18 (left); Kaspars Grinvalds: pages 24–25; andesign101: page 27 (bottom)
Thinkstock: cover (all except bottom, and middle right), pages 4–5, 7 (bottom), 8 (top)
Wikimedia Commons: page 14 (left and right); Gemsling: cover (bottom right), page 6; Phil Whitehorse: page 8 (bottom); H. McKenna: page 9; Cgoodwin: page 10; Maggas: page 11 (bottom); Figaro: page 13 (top); Mattinbgn: page 13 (bottom); John Oxley Library, State Library of Queensland: page 14 (top); Scott Sandars: page 15 (top); Kelisi: page 17 (top); Flying Cloud: page 19; fir0002/flagstaffotos: page 20; John Tann: page 22; National Archives of Australia: page 23 (top); Steve Evans: page 30

Library and Archives Canada Cataloguing in Publication

Aloian, Molly
Cultural traditions in Australia / Molly Aloian.

(Cultural traditions in my world)
Includes index.
Issued also in electronic format.
ISBN 978-0-7787-7516-4 (bound).--ISBN 978-0-7787-7521-8 (pbk.)

1. Festivals--Australia--Juvenile literature. 2. Australia--Social life and customs--Juvenile literature. I. Title. II. Series: Cultural traditions in my world

GT4890.A46 2012   j394.26994   C2012-903964-0

Library of Congress Cataloging-in-Publication Data

Aloian, Molly.
Cultural traditions in Australia / Molly Aloian.
p. cm. -- (Cultural traditions in my world)
Includes index.
ISBN 978-0-7787-7516-4 (reinforced library binding) -- ISBN 978-0-7787-7521-8 (pbk.) -- ISBN 978-1-4271-9040-6 (electronic pdf) -- ISBN 978-1-4271-9094-9 (electronic html)
1. Holidays--Australia--Juvenile literature. 2. Festivals--Australia--Juvenile literature. 3. Australia--Social life and customs--Juvenile literature. I. Title.

GT4890.A46 2013
394.26994--dc23

2012022056

Crabtree Publishing Company

www.crabtreebooks.com   1-800-387-7650

Printed in Hong Kong/092012/BK20120629

Published in Canada
Crabtree Publishing
616 Welland Ave.
St. Catharines, ON
L2M 5V6

Published in the United States
Crabtree Publishing
PMB 59051
350 Fifth Avenue, 59th Floor
New York, New York 10118

Published in the United Kingdom
Crabtree Publishing
Maritime House
Basin Road North, Hove
BN41 1WR

Published in Australia
Crabtree Publishing
3 Charles Street
Coburg North
VIC 3058

Contents

About Australia

Australia is a continent between the Indian Ocean and the Pacific Ocean. The people of Australia have some unique cultural traditions. Cultural traditions are holidays, festivals, special days, and customs that groups of people celebrate each year. **Aboriginal** people brought their traditions to Australia from the continent of Asia thousands of years ago. **Immigrants** from other countries also brought their traditions.

Canberra is the capital of Australia.

Australians still celebrate many of these traditions today. For example, many Chinese people in the city of Sydney celebrate Chinese New Year in January. Some public holidays in Australia are based on the Christian religion. People who follow other religions, such as Buddhism or Islam, celebrate their own cultural traditions.

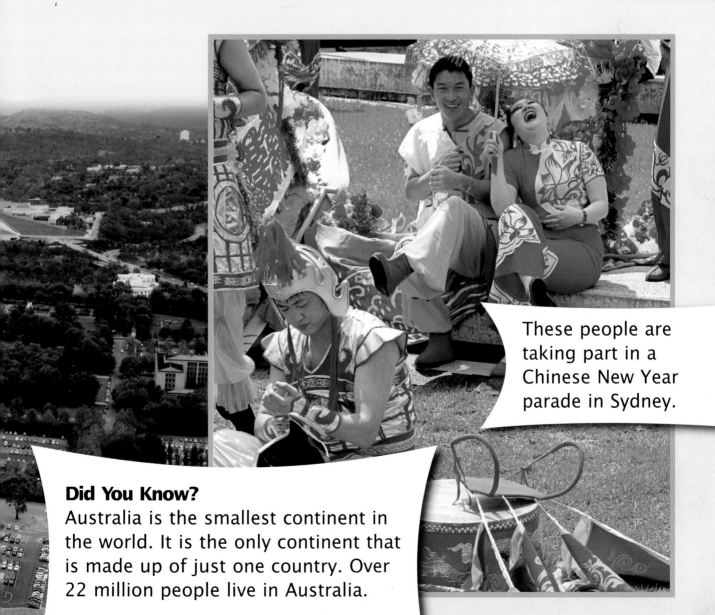

These people are taking part in a Chinese New Year parade in Sydney.

Did You Know?
Australia is the smallest continent in the world. It is the only continent that is made up of just one country. Over 22 million people live in Australia.

Let's Celebrate!

People in Australia celebrate birthdays, weddings, christenings, and other important events just as people do in North America. Many Australian birthday parties are barbecues. Instead of birthday cake, many Australian children eat fairy bread. Fairy bread is sliced white bread cut into triangles or squares, spread with margarine or butter, and topped with colored sprinkles.

Did You Know?

The Aboriginal people who live on the islands in the Torres Strait, in Australia, prepare a popular dish during traditional celebrations. The dish is made of meat and vegetables, such as sweet potato or pumpkin, wrapped in banana or coconut leaves and cooked on hot stones.

fairy bread

6

A 21st birthday is an important birthday in Australia. When a person turns 21, he or she receives a special key. The key is a **symbol** for adulthood and responsibility. Long ago, receiving a key on your 21st birthday meant that you could come and go from your family home whenever you wanted. It is also customary for family and friends to show embarrassing photos or videos of the person who is turning 21.

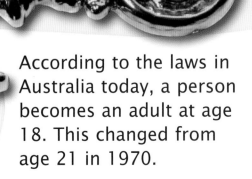

According to the laws in Australia today, a person becomes an adult at age 18. This changed from age 21 in 1970.

Australia Day

On January 26, Australians come together to celebrate their country and the many cultures of the people living in it. Australia was once a British colony. A colony is an area ruled by a faraway country. Australia Day marks the arrival of the **First Fleet** of settlers from Britain at Port Jackson. The First Fleet established the first British settlement on January 26, 1788.

Many events, both on and off the water, take place every year at Sydney Harbor on Australia Day.

Did You Know?
The Australian of the Year Awards take place on Australia Day. These are awards for Australians who have made important contributions to their country or communities.

Ralph Bower Adventureland Park, in Esperance, celebrates Australia Day with children's rides, food, and live music.

Many people have Australia Day off work. They have picnics, barbecues, play or watch sports, and wear green and gold clothing. Green and gold are Australia's national colors. Many families also visit historic sites or museums to learn more about Australia Day, and Australian flags are displayed throughout cities and towns all over Australia.

Easter

In March or April, Australians celebrate Easter with family and friends over a four-day weekend. Many events and festivals take place throughout Australia, including the Fleet Festival in New South Wales, the Sydney Royal Easter Show in Sydney, the National Folk Festival in Australian Capital Territory, and the Australian Gospel Music Festival in Queensland.

Did You Know?
Rabbits were brought to Australia in the 18th century on the First Fleet. Today, rabbits are considered an **invasive** species in Australia. Rabbits cause millions of dollars of damage to crops.

These Shetland ponies are competing in an event at the Sydney Royal Easter Show.

On Easter Sunday, many Australians attend special church services. Children participate in Easter egg hunts, searching for chocolate Easter eggs in parks or gardens. In Australia, the eggs are hidden by the Easter bilby, not the Easter bunny.

A bilby is a type of **marsupial**, with long ears like a rabbit. It lives only in Australia and is an **endangered** species.

At this Greek Orthodox Christian church in Adelaide, members hold candles during the Easter service that are lit by the **priest**.

ANZAC Day

ANZAC Day is a celebration that takes place on April 25 in both Australia and New Zealand. ANZAC stands for the Australian and New Zealand Army Corps. On this day, people honor and remember the soldiers from both countries that fought and died alongside each other defending their countries in past wars.

Did You Know?
An official ANZAC Day ceremony takes place at the Australian War Memorial at 10:15 am. Thousands of people, including the prime minister and the governor general, attend the ceremony.

It is a tradition for the prime minster of Australia to give a speech on ANZAC Day.

On ANZAC Day, special services are held at dawn. Later in the day, former soldiers take part in marches throughout the major cities and in many smaller communities. People attend **commemorative** ceremonies at war memorials. They listen to speeches, say prayers, and lay wreaths on monuments and on soldiers' tombstones.

Wreaths are laid at The Gap War Memorial in Brisbane for ANZAC Day (above). Former soldiers, known as **veterans**, participate in a march on ANZAC Day in Melbourne.

Labor Day

Labor Day is a public holiday in many places throughout Australia. Labor Day celebrates the many workers who have contributed to Australia's **economy**. It also commemorates the beginning of the eight-hour workday for Australians. In the past, people had to work 12 or more hours a day in extremely harsh conditions.

Meatworkers celebrate the eight-hour working day in 1910.

Did You Know?
Labor Day is also known as Eight Hours Day and May Day.

8 HOURS LABOUR
8 HOURS RECREATION
8 HOURS REST

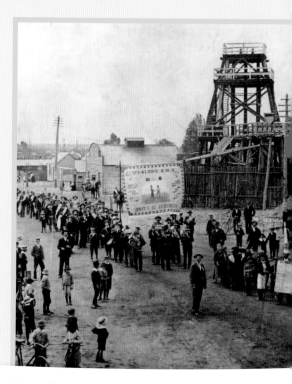

The first Labor Day marches were held in 1891.

Eight Hour monument

The number eight is on many union buildings throughout Australia as a symbol of the eight-hour workday. In 1903, a monument featuring a golden globe and the numbers 888 was built in Melbourne to celebrate the movement. It is called the Eight Hour monument. The three eights represent eight hours of work, eight hours of rest, and eight hours of recreation.

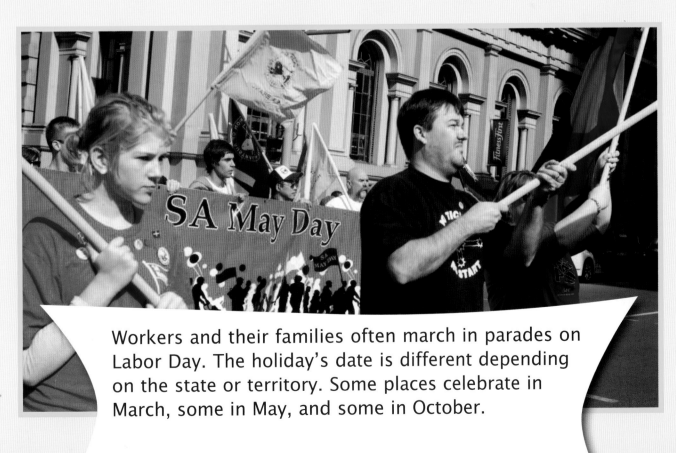

Workers and their families often march in parades on Labor Day. The holiday's date is different depending on the state or territory. Some places celebrate in March, some in May, and some in October.

Mabo Day

Mabo Day is on June 3 each year. On this day, people in Queensland, Australia, remember and honor a Torres Strait Islander named Eddie Koiki Mabo (1936-1992). Mabo fought for the rights of Aboriginal peoples, especially their rights to land that had been taken from them by British settlers. In 2010, a campaign was launched to make Mabo Day a national holiday in Australia.

On August 22, 1770, British explorer James Cook raised the British flag on Possession Island in the Torres Strait. He claimed the east coast as British terrority and named it New South Wales.

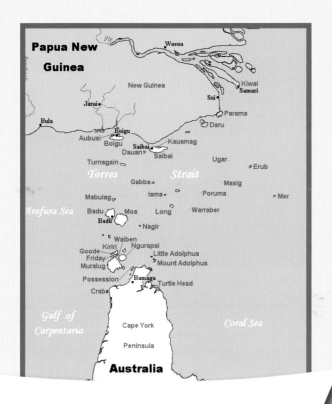

On Mabo Day, people are encouraged to reflect on the damage **colonization** caused to the lives of Aboriginal Australians. It is a day for **reconciliation** and forgiveness and is meant to unite Aboriginal and non-Aboriginal Australian people.

Did You Know?
The Torres Strait Islands are a group of over 270 islands in the Torres Strait, which is a waterway between Australia and Papa New Guinea. Torres Strait Islanders are Aboriginal people from these islands.

Torres Strait Island dancers wear a traditional white headdress called a *dhari*.

Queen's Birthday

In most of Australia, people celebrate the Queen's birthday on the second Monday in June. In Western Australia, people celebrate the Queen's birthday in October. Many Australians spend the day off with their families and friends playing or watching sports and having picnics or barbecues.

Did You Know?
Australia is a member of the **Commonwealth of Nations** and Queen Elizabeth II is the official head of state.

Queen Elizabeth II is on many Australian coins.

One well-known sports event that takes place on the Queen's birthday is an AFL (Australian Football League) game between the Collingwood Magpies and the Melbourne Demons. The teams play at the Melbourne Cricket Club, the largest and oldest sports club in Australia.

The Melbourne Demons huddle during the AFL game on the Queen's birthday. Australian football is similar to European soccer, but with different rules.

Ekka Day

There are agricultural shows throughout Australia, but one of the largest shows takes place in Brisbane, the capital city of Queensland. Ekka Day, also known as the Royal National Agricultural Show Day, is usually on the second Wednesday in August. While this one day has become a public holiday in the Brisbane area, the show lasts for over a week.

Each Australian state has its own agricultural "Royal Show." The Royal Shows are usually the largest agricultural shows in the state. Victoria hosts the Royal Melbourne Show every September.

Farmers, breeders, and spectators come to the Ekka show to learn about new farming equipment, show off their crops and animals, and compete in events. There are awards for young people, too! The Rural Achievers Award goes to a young person who is involved in agriculture in his or her community. The show attracts over 600,000 people each year from Australia and around the world.

Did You Know?
The Royal National Agricultural Show also features fireworks displays, games, amusement park rides, parades, food, and crafts.

The super long Euro Slide is a popular ride at the Ekka show.

National Wattle Day

The first day in September is National Wattle Day in Australia. The golden wattle—a green and gold flower that blooms in spring—is Australia's official floral **emblem**. There are close to 1,000 different species of wattles, almost all of which are found only in Australia.

Did You Know?
Wattles are among the first plants to begin to grow after a fire or flood. They help to enrich the soil. Wattles are a symbol of renewal and **resilience**.

Australia's coat of arms features wattle branches. A coat of arms is a design that identifies a country or group.

On this day, Australians celebrate the natural environment and all the plants and animals living in it. People wear pieces of wattle plants to remind themselves and others of the importance of preserving Australia's fragile rainforests, deserts, and bushlands, so that future generations can enjoy them for years to come.

Melbourne Cup Day

The first Tuesday of November is Melbourne Cup Day. On this day, Australians watch a horse race called the Melbourne Cup that is held at the Flemington Racecourse in Melbourne. The race is often called "the race that stops a nation" because nearly everyone stops what they are doing to watch the two-mile (3.2 km) race on television or listen to it on the radio.

Did You Know?
Melbourne Cup Day has been an official public holiday in Melbourne since 1877.

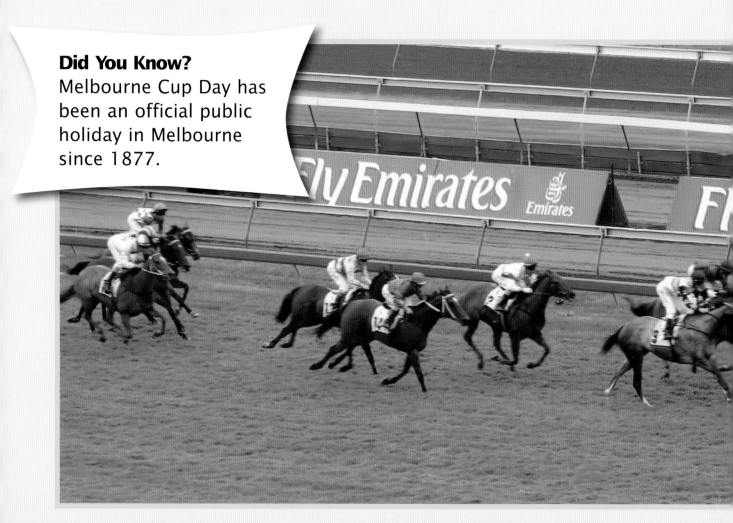

More than 100,000 people usually attend the race at Flemington Racecourse. Many people dress up. Women wear their best or most colorful hats and dresses. Local, national, and international celebrities also attend the race and make sure they show off their unique outfits.

Christmas

Many Australians celebrate Christmas on December 25. In December, it is the middle of summer in Australia. People decorate their homes with lights and hang ornaments from pine trees. Family members exchange gifts and visit relatives and neighbors. At lunchtime, families and friends gather together and eat turkey or roast lamb, potatoes, gravy, baked vegetables, pies, and puddings. Some people barbecue seafood.

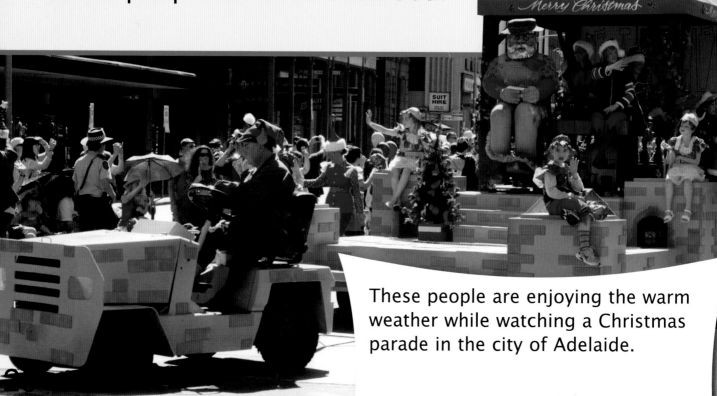

These people are enjoying the warm weather while watching a Christmas parade in the city of Adelaide.

One Australian Christmas treat is called Christmas damper. It is a type of homemade soda bread baked in the shape of a star or a Christmas tree and decorated with holly. People serve it with butter, honey, jam, or syrup.

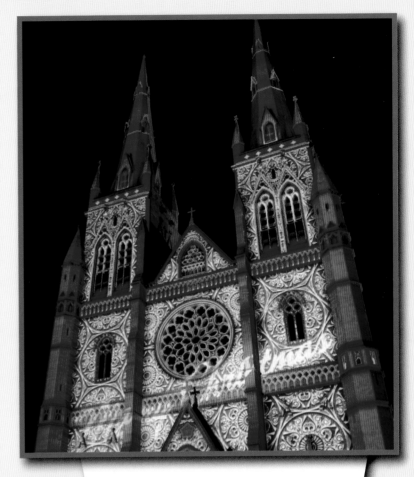

St Mary's Cathedral in Sydney becomes a painting of light, as different colorful patterns and words, such as "Merry Christmas," are projected onto the building.

The annual Variety Santa Fun Run held in major cities across Australia, features participants dressed in Santa suits running to raise money for children in need at Christmas.

New Year's Eve

New Year's Eve is on December 31. Many Australians celebrate New Year's Eve with music, parties, parades, and other forms of entertainment. Over one million people watch the fireworks display at Sydney Harbor. There are fireworks displays in smaller towns and cities, too.

The fireworks at Sydney Harbor have themes each year. In 2011, the theme was "Time to Dream." It was to inspire people to pursue their dreams in the new year. Fireworks were set off in the shapes of clouds because, as the old saying goes, "every cloud has a silver lining."

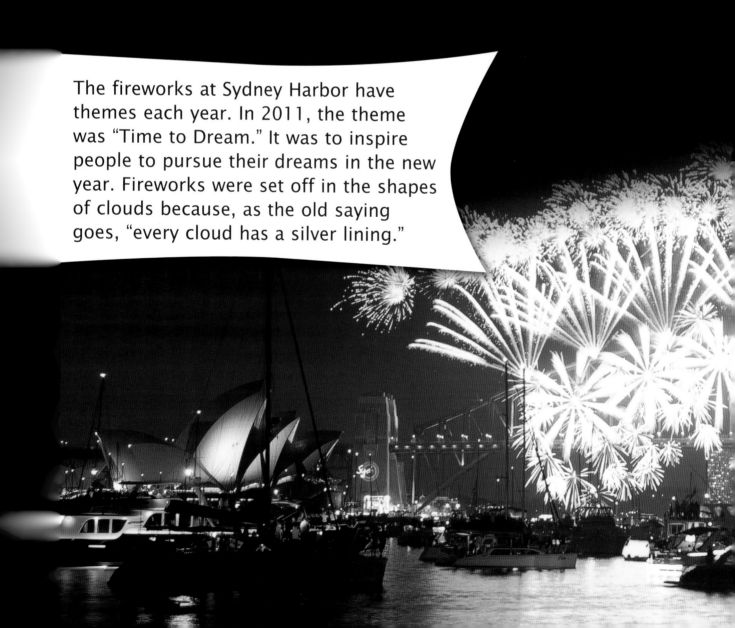

On New Year's Day, many people get together with friends and family and watch a popular thoroughbred horse race, called the Perth Cup, on television. The race takes place at the Ascot Racecourse in Perth, and is just over two miles (3.2 km) long. The race has been run since 1887. People bet on the horse they think will win the race.

Did You Know?
New Year's Day is a public holiday in Australia.

Aboriginal Festivals

Each year, there are more than 100 festivals that celebrate Aboriginal culture and history in Australia. The Dreaming Festival, in Queensland, is one of the largest Aboriginal festivals in Australia. It started in 2004 and features traditional healing, art, rituals, food, and story circles. The Torres Strait Cultural Festival celebrates the songs, food, and art of Torres Strait Islanders.

Did You Know?
The Dreaming or the Dreamtime is an important part of Aboriginal culture. For Aboriginal people, the Dreamtime is the story of the creation of the world.

Many Aboriginal festivals feature music from the traditional Aboriginal musical instrument, the didgeridoo.

The Laura Aboriginal Dance Festival is a three-day event that celebrates the languages, songs, dances, and stories of Aboriginal people in the town of Laura.

These Aboriginal men are performing a traditional dance at the Aboriginal Dance Festival in the city of Laura.

Glossary

Aboriginal The first people in an area or region

colonization Establishing a colony

commemorative To act as a reminder of something; to remember or honor

Commonwealth of Nations The United Kingdom and most of the countries that are linked to it

economy Relating to a country's production, distribution, and consumption of goods and services

emblem An object or item that stands for or represents an idea

endangered Describes animals that are in danger of dying out in the wild

First Fleet Eleven British ships carrying about 1,350 people that landed in Australia in 1788 and established the first colony

immigrants People who come to live in a new country

invasive Tending to spread

marsupial A type of mammal that carries its babies in a pouch

priest Leader of a Greek Orthodox church

reconciliation Forgiving wrongdoing and becoming friendly again

resilience Being able to recover quickly or easily adjust to change

symbol Something that stands for something else

veteran A person who has served in the armed forces

Index